One Earth, a Multitude of Creatures

Peter and Connie Roop

Illustrations by Valerie A. Kells

Walker and Company
New York

For Bobby—whose interest in animal group names inspired our book.

—Peter and Connie Roop

For Drew, may the birds in the sky and the whales in the sea bring to you the joy they brought to me.

—Valerie A. Kells

The authors thank Jim Anderson, naturalist at Mosquito Hill Nature Center, for his invaluable assistance with this book. Jim is one of a kind, a "natural" teacher. Peter and Connie also thank Bev Bush, who so willingly shares her English expertise.

First published in the United States of America in 1992
by Walker Publishing Company, Inc.

Published simultaneously in Canada by Thomas Allen & Son
Canada, Limited, Markham, Ontario

Library of Congress Cataloging-in-Publication Data
Roop, Peter.
One earth, a multitude of creatures / Peter and Connie Roop; illustrations by Valerie A. Kells.
p.   cm.
Summary: Introduces animals that are a part of the ecosystem of the Pacific Northwest, discussing how they depend on one another and their environment for survival.
ISBN 0-8027-8192-6.   —ISBN 0-8027-8193-4
1. Zoology—Northwest, Pacific—Juvenile literature.
[1. Zoology—Northwest, Pacific.] I. Roop, Connie. II. Kells, Valerie A., ill.   III. Title.
QL155.R66   1992
591.9795—dc20   92-14057
                                                            CIP
                                                            AC

Animals / Species list compiled by Valerie A. Kells

Printed in the United States of America

10 9 8 7 6 5 4 3 2 1

One Earth, a Multitude of Creatures features
animals that are part of just one of many of the
Earth's ecosystems, the Pacific Northwest. Animals
are dependent on one another and their
environment for survival. A healthy environment is
necessary for a multitude of creatures to survive.
As individuals and as groups, all animals are part of
the circle of life on our one Earth.

In the light of the full moon, an owl swoops down and catches a mouse as a staring of owls watches a fox.

A mother fox, sensing danger, signals to her litter of pups to slip into the den.

As the sky brightens at dawn, the sentinel raven caws as an unkindness of ravens bullies an awakening hawk.

Over in the meadow, one honey bee lingers on a flower while a swarm of bees returns to the hive.

A determined bear rocks the hollow tree while a sleuth of bears traps trout in the stream.

At noon, sunlight sparkles on a trout leaping for lunch as a hover of trout waits in a deep pool.

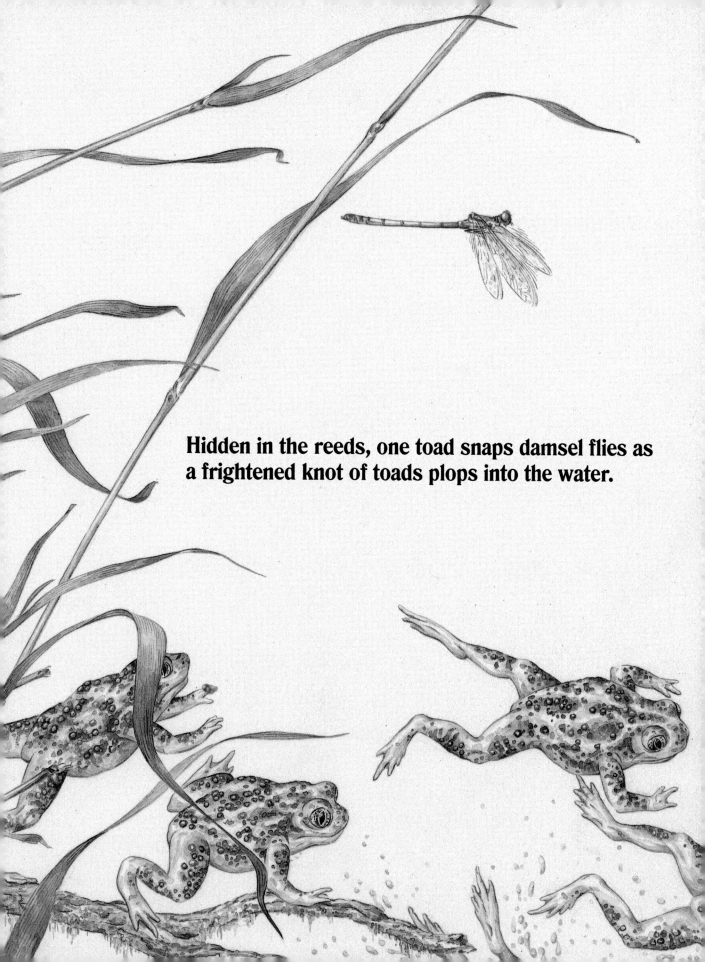

Hidden in the reeds, one toad snaps damsel flies as a frightened knot of toads plops into the water.

One fat caterpillar rests beneath a leaf as an army of caterpillars creeps down the willow branches.

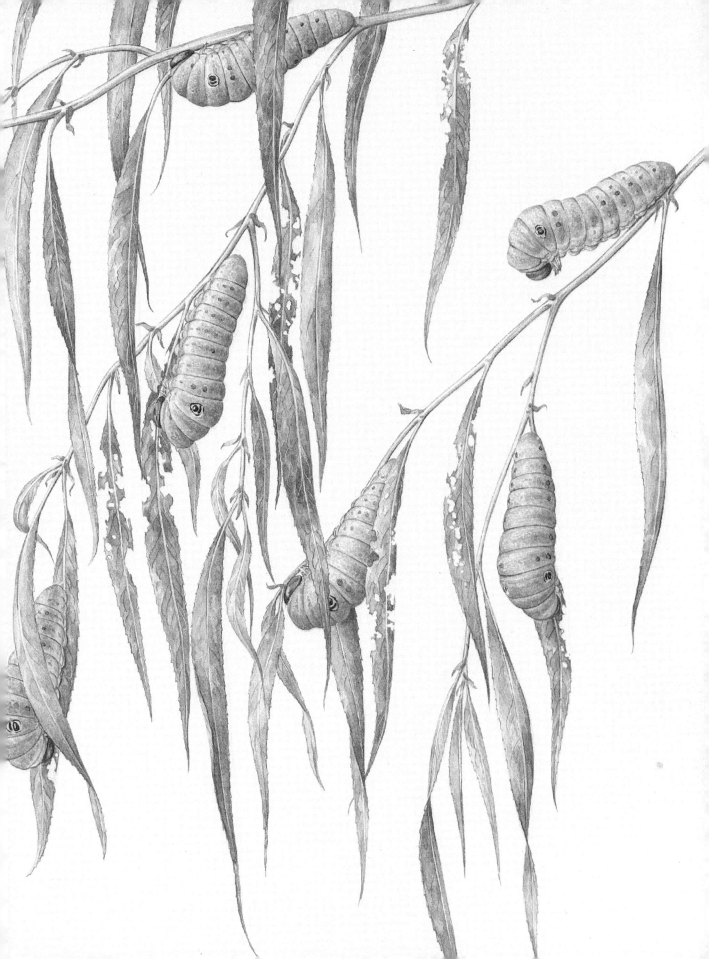

At the edge of the meadow, a lark snatches the caterpillar as an exaltation of larks bursts from a bush.

One clam snaps its shell as a bed of clams burrows
to escape the waves made by a hungry gull.

Riding a breeze, the gull drops a clam, cracking it open, as a flock of gulls follows a fishing boat out to sea.

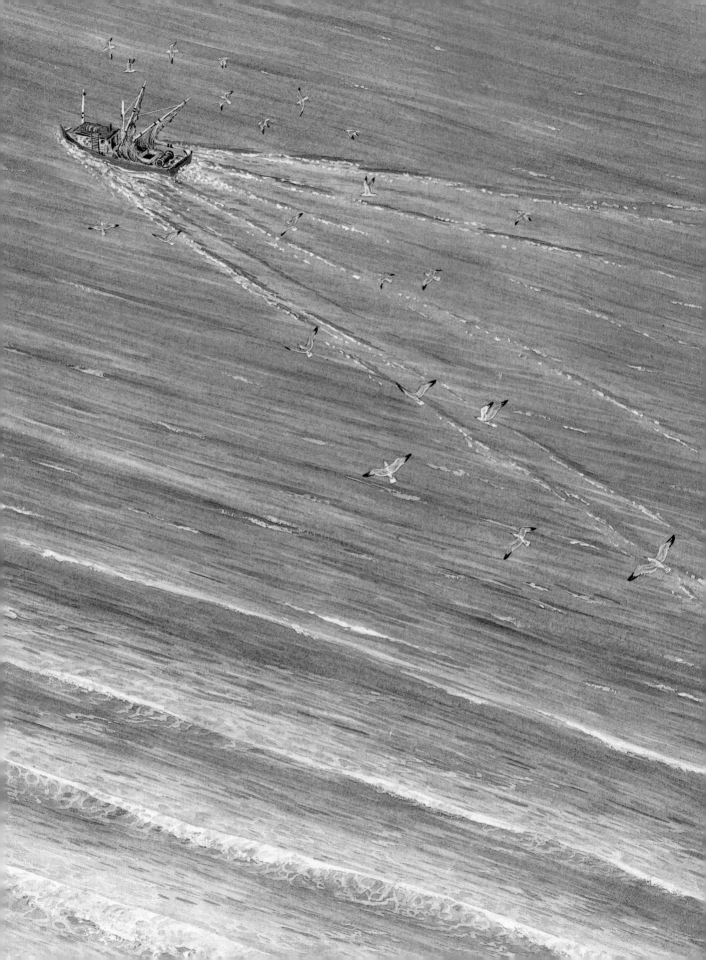

As the sun sets, a whale breaches before joining its pod.

A jellyfish stings tiny shrimp with its tentacles as a smack of jellyfish pulses with the incoming tide.

In the light of the full moon, a staring of owls watches as the waves roll in.

Animals/Species in This Book

Barn Owl— *Tyto alba*

Black Bear— *Ursus americanus*

Dark Lestes Damselfly— *Lestes congener*

Gray Fox— *Urocyon cinereoargenteus*

Green Sea Turtle—Chelonia mydas

Herring Gull— *Larus argentatus*

Honey Bee— *Apis mellifera*

Horned Lark— *Eremophila alpestris*

Humpback Whale— *Megaptera novaeangliae*

Pacific Razor Clam— *Siliqua patula*

Purple-striped Jellyfish— *Pelagia colorata*

Rainbow Trout— *Salmo gairdneri*

Raven— *Corvus corax*

Red-tailed Hawk— *Buteo jamaicensis*

Spring Azure Butterfly— *Celastrina argiolus*

Streak-winged Red Skimmer Dragonfly—
Sympetrum illotum

Western Spadefoot Toad— *Scaphiopus
hammondii*

Western Tiger Swallowtail Caterpillar—
Papilio rutulus